Internet Addresses and Accounts
By
Catherine Coulter

ISBN-13: 978-1484197998

ISBN-10: 1484197992

You can add a category or numbers to the pages if you wish to. If you want to put your web sites in alphabetical order you can do that as well. The way you organize your web sites in this book is up to you.

Category_____

Category_____

Category_____

Category_____

Category_____

Category_____

Category_____

Category_____

Category_____

Category_____

Category_____ Page_____

Web Site:

User Name	Password	$	Day Monthly Yearly	Start Date	End Date

Web Site:

User Name	Password	$	Day Monthly Yearly	Start Date	End Date

Web Site:

User Name	Password	$	Day Monthly Yearly	Start Date	End Date

Web Site:

User Name	Password	$	Day Monthly Yearly	Start Date	End Date

Web Site:

User Name	Password	$	Day Monthly Yearly	Start Date	End Date

Web Site:

User Name	Password	$	Day Monthly Yearly	Start Date	End Date

Web Site:

User Name	Password	$	Day Monthly Yearly	Start Date	End Date

Category_____ **Page**_____

Web Site:					
User Name	**Password**	**$**	**Day Monthly Yearly**	**Start Date**	**End Date**

Web Site:					
User Name	**Password**	**$**	**Day Monthly Yearly**	**Start Date**	**End Date**

Web Site:					
User Name	**Password**	**$**	**Day Monthly Yearly**	**Start Date**	**End Date**

Web Site:					
User Name	**Password**	**$**	**Day Monthly Yearly**	**Start Date**	**End Date**

Web Site:					
User Name	**Password**	**$**	**Day Monthly Yearly**	**Start Date**	**End Date**

Web Site:					
User Name	**Password**	**$**	**Day Monthly Yearly**	**Start Date**	**End Date**

Web Site:					
User Name	**Password**	**$**	**Day Monthly Yearly**	**Start Date**	**End Date**

Category_____ **Page**_____

Web Site:					
User Name	Password	$	Day Monthly Yearly	Start Date	End Date

Web Site:					
User Name	Password	$	Day Monthly Yearly	Start Date	End Date

Web Site:					
User Name	Password	$	Day Monthly Yearly	Start Date	End Date

Web Site:					
User Name	Password	$	Day Monthly Yearly	Start Date	End Date

Web Site:					
User Name	Password	$	Day Monthly Yearly	Start Date	End Date

Web Site:					
User Name	Password	$	Day Monthly Yearly	Start Date	End Date

Web Site:					
User Name	Password	$	Day Monthly Yearly	Start Date	End Date

Category_____ **Page**_____

Web Site:

User Name	Password	$	Day Monthly Yearly	Start Date	End Date

Web Site:

User Name	Password	$	Day Monthly Yearly	Start Date	End Date

Web Site:

User Name	Password	$	Day Monthly Yearly	Start Date	End Date

Web Site:

User Name	Password	$	Day Monthly Yearly	Start Date	End Date

Web Site:

User Name	Password	$	Day Monthly Yearly	Start Date	End Date

Web Site:

User Name	Password	$	Day Monthly Yearly	Start Date	End Date

Web Site:

User Name	Password	$	Day Monthly Yearly	Start Date	End Date

Category _____ **Page**_____

Web Site:					
User Name	**Password**	**$**	**Day Monthly Yearly**	**Start Date**	**End Date**

Web Site:					
User Name	**Password**	**$**	**Day Monthly Yearly**	**Start Date**	**End Date**

Web Site:					
User Name	**Password**	**$**	**Day Monthly Yearly**	**Start Date**	**End Date**

Web Site:					
User Name	**Password**	**$**	**Day Monthly Yearly**	**Start Date**	**End Date**

Web Site:					
User Name	**Password**	**$**	**Day Monthly Yearly**	**Start Date**	**End Date**

Web Site:					
User Name	**Password**	**$**	**Day Monthly Yearly**	**Start Date**	**End Date**

Web Site:					
User Name	**Password**	**$**	**Day Monthly Yearly**	**Start Date**	**End Date**

Category_____ **Page**_____

Web Site:					
User Name	Password	$	Day Monthly Yearly	Start Date	End Date

Web Site:					
User Name	Password	$	Day Monthly Yearly	Start Date	End Date

Web Site:					
User Name	Password	$	Day Monthly Yearly	Start Date	End Date

Web Site:					
User Name	Password	$	Day Monthly Yearly	Start Date	End Date

Web Site:					
User Name	Password	$	Day Monthly Yearly	Start Date	End Date

Web Site:					
User SName	Password	$	Day Monthly Yearly	Start Date	End Date

Web Site:					
User Name	Password	$	Day Monthly Yearly	Start Date	End Date

Category_____ **Page**_____

Web Site:					
User Name	**Password**	**$**	**Day Monthly Yearly**	**Start Date**	**End Date**

Web Site:					
User Name	**Password**	**$**	**Day Monthly Yearly**	**Start Date**	**End Date**

Web Site:					
User Name	**Password**	**$**	**Day Monthly Yearly**	**Start Date**	**End Date**

Web Site:					
User Name	**Password**	**$**	**Day Monthly Yearly**	**Start Date**	**End Date**

Web Site:					
User Name	**Password**	**$**	**Day Monthly Yearly**	**Start Date**	**End Date**

Web Site:					
User Name	**Password**	**$**	**Day Monthly Yearly**	**Start Date**	**End Date**

Web Site:					
User Name	**Password**	**$**	**Day Monthly Yearly**	**Start Date**	**End Date**

Category_____ **Page**_____

Web Site:					
User Name	Password	$	Day Monthly Yearly	Start Date	End Date

Web Site:					
User Name	Password	$	Day Monthly Yearly	Start Date	End Date

Web Site:					
User Name	Password	$	Day Monthly Yearly	Start Date	End Date

Web Site:					
User Name	Password	$	Day Monthly Yearly	Start Date	End Date

Web Site:					
User Name	Password	$	Day Monthly Yearly	Start Date	End Date

Web Site:					
User Name	Password	$	Day Monthly Yearly	Start Date	End Date

Web Site:					
User Name	Password	$	Day Monthly Yearly	Start Date	End Date

Category_____ **Page**_____

Web Site:					
User Name	**Password**	**$**	**Day Monthly Yearly**	**Start Date**	**End Date**

Web Site:					
User Name	**Password**	**$**	**Day Monthly Yearly**	**Start Date**	**End Date**

Web Site:					
User Name	**Password**	**$**	**Day Monthly Yearly**	**Start Date**	**End Date**

Web Site:					
User Name	**Password**	**$**	**Day Monthly Yearly**	**Start Date**	**End Date**

Web Site:					
User Name	**Password**	**$**	**Day Monthly Yearly**	**Start Date**	**End Date**

Web Site:					
User SName	**Password**	**$**	**Day Monthly Yearly**	**Start Date**	**End Date**

Web Site:					
User Name	**Password**	**$**	**Day Monthly Yearly**	**Start Date**	**End Date**

Category_____ **Page**_____

Web Site:

User Name	Password	$	Day Monthly Yearly	Start Date	End Date

Web Site:

User Name	Password	$	Day Monthly Yearly	Start Date	End Date

Web Site:

User Name	Password	$	Day Monthly Yearly	Start Date	End Date

Web Site:

User Name	Password	$	Day Monthly Yearly	Start Date	End Date

Web Site:

User Name	Password	$	Day Monthly Yearly	Start Date	End Date

Web Site:

User SName	Password	$	Day Monthly Yearly	Start Date	End Date

Web Site:

User Name	Password	$	Day Monthly Yearly	Start Date	End Date

Category_____ Page_____

Web Site:

User Name	Password	$	Day Monthly Yearly	Start Date	End Date

Web Site:

User Name	Password	$	Day Monthly Yearly	Start Date	End Date

Web Site:

User Name	Password	$	Day Monthly Yearly	Start Date	End Date

Web Site:

User Name	Password	$	Day Monthly Yearly	Start Date	End Date

Web Site:

User Name	Password	$	Day Monthly Yearly	Start Date	End Date

Web Site:

User Name	Password	$	Day Monthly Yearly	Start Date	End Date

Web Site:

User Name	Password	$	Day Monthly Yearly	Start Date	End Date

Category_____ **Page**_____

Web Site:

User Name	Password	$	Day Monthly Yearly	Start Date	End Date

Web Site:

User Name	Password	$	Day Monthly Yearly	Start Date	End Date

Web Site:

User Name	Password	$	Day Monthly Yearly	Start Date	End Date

Web Site:

User Name	Password	$	Day Monthly Yearly	Start Date	End Date

Web Site:

User Name	Password	$	Day Monthly Yearly	Start Date	End Date

Web Site:

User Name	Password	$	Day Monthly Yearly	Start Date	End Date

Web Site:

User Name	Password	$	Day Monthly Yearly	Start Date	End Date

Category_____ Page_____

Web Site:

User Name	Password	$	Day Monthly Yearly	Start Date	End Date

Web Site:

User Name	Password	$	Day Monthly Yearly	Start Date	End Date

Web Site:

User Name	Password	$	Day Monthly Yearly	Start Date	End Date

Web Site:

User Name	Password	$	Day Monthly Yearly	Start Date	End Date

Web Site:

User Name	Password	$	Day Monthly Yearly	Start Date	End Date

Web Site:

User Name	Password	$	Day Monthly Yearly	Start Date	End Date

Web Site:

User Name	Password	$	Day Monthly Yearly	Start Date	End Date

Category_____ **Page**_____

Web Site:					
User Name	Password	$	Day Monthly Yearly	Start Date	End Date

Web Site:					
User Name	Password	$	Day Monthly Yearly	Start Date	End Date

Web Site:					
User Name	Password	$	Day Monthly Yearly	Start Date	End Date

Web Site:					
User Name	Password	$	Day Monthly Yearly	Start Date	End Date

Web Site:					
User Name	Password	$	Day Monthly Yearly	Start Date	End Date

Web Site:					
User Name	Password	$	Day Monthly Yearly	Start Date	End Date

Web Site:					
User Name	Password	$	Day Monthly Yearly	Start Date	End Date

Category_____ Page_____

Web Site:

User Name	Password	$	Day Monthly Yearly	Start Date	End Date

Web Site:

User Name	Password	$	Day Monthly Yearly	Start Date	End Date

Web Site:

User Name	Password	$	Day Monthly Yearly	Start Date	End Date

Web Site:

User Name	Password	$	Day Monthly Yearly	Start Date	End Date

Web Site:

User Name	Password	$	Day Monthly Yearly	Start Date	End Date

Web Site:

User Name	Password	$	Day Monthly Yearly	Start Date	End Date

Web Site:

User Name	Password	$	Day Monthly Yearly	Start Date	End Date

Category_____ **Page**_____

Web Site:

User Name	Password	$	Day Monthly Yearly	Start Date	End Date

Web Site:

User Name	Password	$	Day Monthly Yearly	Start Date	End Date

Web Site:

User Name	Password	$	Day Monthly Yearly	Start Date	End Date

Web Site:

User Name	Password	$	Day Monthly Yearly	Start Date	End Date

Web Site:

User Name	Password	$	Day Monthly Yearly	Start Date	End Date

Web Site:

User Name	Password	$	Day Monthly Yearly	Start Date	End Date

Web Site:

User Name	Password	$	Day Monthly Yearly	Start Date	End Date

Category_____ Page_____

Web Site:

User Name	Password	$	Day Monthly Yearly	Start Date	End Date

Web Site:

User Name	Password	$	Day Monthly Yearly	Start Date	End Date

Web Site:

User Name	Password	$	Day Monthly Yearly	Start Date	End Date

Web Site:

User Name	Password	$	Day Monthly Yearly	Start Date	End Date

Web Site:

User Name	Password	$	Day Monthly Yearly	Start Date	End Date

Web Site:

User Name	Password	$	Day Monthly Yearly	Start Date	End Date

Web Site:

User Name	Password	$	Day Monthly Yearly	Start Date	End Date

Category_____ **Page**_____

Web Site:

User Name	Password	$	Day Monthly Yearly	Start Date	End Date

Web Site:

User Name	Password	$	Day Monthly Yearly	Start Date	End Date

Web Site:

User Name	Password	$	Day Monthly Yearly	Start Date	End Date

Web Site:

User Name	Password	$	Day Monthly Yearly	Start Date	End Date

Web Site:

User Name	Password	$	Day Monthly Yearly	Start Date	End Date

Web Site:

User Name	Password	$	Day Monthly Yearly	Start Date	End Date

Web Site:

User Name	Password	$	Day Monthly Yearly	Start Date	End Date

Category_____ **Page**_____

Web Site:

User Name	Password	$	Day Monthly Yearly	Start Date	End Date

Web Site:

User Name	Password	$	Day Monthly Yearly	Start Date	End Date

Web Site:

User Name	Password	$	Day Monthly Yearly	Start Date	End Date

Web Site:

User Name	Password	$	Day Monthly Yearly	Start Date	End Date

Web Site:

User Name	Password	$	Day Monthly Yearly	Start Date	End Date

Web Site:

User Name	Password	$	Day Monthly Yearly	Start Date	End Date

Web Site:

User Name	Password	$	Day Monthly Yearly	Start Date	End Date

Category_____ Page_____

Web Site:

User Name	Password	$	Day Monthly Yearly	Start Date	End Date

Web Site:

User Name	Password	$	Day Monthly Yearly	Start Date	End Date

Web Site:

User Name	Password	$	Day Monthly Yearly	Start Date	End Date

Web Site:

User Name	Password	$	Day Monthly Yearly	Start Date	End Date

Web Site:

User Name	Password	$	Day Monthly Yearly	Start Date	End Date

Web Site:

User Name	Password	$	Day Monthly Yearly	Start Date	End Date

Web Site:

User Name	Password	$	Day Monthly Yearly	Start Date	End Date

Category_____ **Page**_____

Web Site:					
User Name	Password	$	Day Monthly Yearly	Start Date	End Date

Web Site:					
User Name	Password	$	Day Monthly Yearly	Start Date	End Date

Web Site:					
User Name	Password	$	Day Monthly Yearly	Start Date	End Date

Web Site:					
User Name	Password	$	Day Monthly Yearly	Start Date	End Date

Web Site:					
User Name	Password	$	Day Monthly Yearly	Start Date	End Date

Web Site:					
User Name	Password	$	Day Monthly Yearly	Start Date	End Date

Web Site:					
User Name	Password	$	Day Monthly Yearly	Start Date	End Date

Category_____ Page_____

Web Site:

User Name	Password	$	Day Monthly Yearly	Start Date	End Date

Web Site:

User Name	Password	$	Day Monthly Yearly	Start Date	End Date

Web Site:

User Name	Password	$	Day Monthly Yearly	Start Date	End Date

Web Site:

User Name	Password	$	Day Monthly Yearly	Start Date	End Date

Web Site:

User Name	Password	$	Day Monthly Yearly	Start Date	End Date

Web Site:

User Name	Password	$	Day Monthly Yearly	Start Date	End Date

Web Site:

User Name	Password	$	Day Monthly Yearly	Start Date	End Date

Category_____ **Page**_____

Web Site:

User Name	Password	$	Day Monthly Yearly	Start Date	End Date

Web Site:

User Name	Password	$	Day Monthly Yearly	Start Date	End Date

Web Site:

User Name	Password	$	Day Monthly Yearly	Start Date	End Date

Web Site:

User Name	Password	$	Day Monthly Yearly	Start Date	End Date

Web Site:

User Name	Password	$	Day Monthly Yearly	Start Date	End Date

Web Site:

User Name	Password	$	Day Monthly Yearly	Start Date	End Date

Web Site:

User Name	Password	$	Day Monthly Yearly	Start Date	End Date

Category_____ Page_____

Web Site:

User Name	Password	$	Day Monthly Yearly	Start Date	End Date

Web Site:

User Name	Password	$	Day Monthly Yearly	Start Date	End Date

Web Site:

User Name	Password	$	Day Monthly Yearly	Start Date	End Date

Web Site:

User Name	Password	$	Day Monthly Yearly	Start Date	End Date

Web Site:

User Name	Password	$	Day Monthly Yearly	Start Date	End Date

Web Site:

User Name	Password	$	Day Monthly Yearly	Start Date	End Date

Web Site:

User Name	Password	$	Day Monthly Yearly	Start Date	End Date

Category_____ **Page**_____

Web Site:

User Name	Password	$	Day Monthly Yearly	Start Date	End Date

Web Site:

User Name	Password	$	Day Monthly Yearly	Start Date	End Date

Web Site:

User Name	Password	$	Day Monthly Yearly	Start Date	End Date

Web Site:

User Name	Password	$	Day Monthly Yearly	Start Date	End Date

Web Site:

User Name	Password	$	Day Monthly Yearly	Start Date	End Date

Web Site:

User Name	Password	$	Day Monthly Yearly	Start Date	End Date

Web Site:

User Name	Password	$	Day Monthly Yearly	Start Date	End Date

Category_____ Page_____

Web Site:

User Name	Password	$	Day Monthly Yearly	Start Date	End Date

Web Site:

User Name	Password	$	Day Monthly Yearly	Start Date	End Date

Web Site:

User Name	Password	$	Day Monthly Yearly	Start Date	End Date

Web Site:

User Name	Password	$	Day Monthly Yearly	Start Date	End Date

Web Site:

User Name	Password	$	Day Monthly Yearly	Start Date	End Date

Web Site:

User Name	Password	$	Day Monthly Yearly	Start Date	End Date

Web Site:

User Name	Password	$	Day Monthly Yearly	Start Date	End Date

Category_____ **Page**_____

Web Site:

User Name	Password	$	Day Monthly Yearly	Start Date	End Date

Web Site:

User Name	Password	$	Day Monthly Yearly	Start Date	End Date

Web Site:

User Name	Password	$	Day Monthly Yearly	Start Date	End Date

Web Site:

User Name	Password	$	Day Monthly Yearly	Start Date	End Date

Web Site:

User Name	Password	$	Day Monthly Yearly	Start Date	End Date

Web Site:

User Name	Password	$	Day Monthly Yearly	Start Date	End Date

Web Site:

User Name	Password	$	Day Monthly Yearly	Start Date	End Date

Category_____ **Page**_____

Web Site:

User Name	Password	$	Day Monthly Yearly	Start Date	End Date

Web Site:

User Name	Password	$	Day Monthly Yearly	Start Date	End Date

Web Site:

User Name	Password	$	Day Monthly Yearly	Start Date	End Date

Web Site:

User Name	Password	$	Day Monthly Yearly	Start Date	End Date

Web Site:

User Name	Password	$	Day Monthly Yearly	Start Date	End Date

Web Site:

User Name	Password	$	Day Monthly Yearly	Start Date	End Date

Web Site:

User Name	Password	$	Day Monthly Yearly	Start Date	End Date

Category_____ **Page**_____

Web Site:

User Name	Password	$	Day Monthly Yearly	Start Date	End Date

Web Site:

User Name	Password	$	Day Monthly Yearly	Start Date	End Date

Web Site:

User Name	Password	$	Day Monthly Yearly	Start Date	End Date

Web Site:

User Name	Password	$	Day Monthly Yearly	Start Date	End Date

Web Site:

User Name	Password	$	Day Monthly Yearly	Start Date	End Date

Web Site:

User Name	Password	$	Day Monthly Yearly	Start Date	End Date

Web Site:

User Name	Password	$	Day Monthly Yearly	Start Date	End Date

Category_____ Page_____

Web Site:

User Name	Password	$	Day Monthly Yearly	Start Date	End Date

Web Site:

User Name	Password	$	Day Monthly Yearly	Start Date	End Date

Web Site:

User Name	Password	$	Day Monthly Yearly	Start Date	End Date

Web Site:

User Name	Password	$	Day Monthly Yearly	Start Date	End Date

Web Site:

User Name	Password	$	Day Monthly Yearly	Start Date	End Date

Web Site:

User Name	Password	$	Day Monthly Yearly	Start Date	End Date

Web Site:

User Name	Password	$	Day Monthly Yearly	Start Date	End Date

Category_____ **Page**_____

Web Site:

User Name	Password	$	Day Monthly Yearly	Start Date	End Date

Web Site:

User Name	Password	$	Day Monthly Yearly	Start Date	End Date

Web Site:

User Name	Password	$	Day Monthly Yearly	Start Date	End Date

Web Site:

User Name	Password	$	Day Monthly Yearly	Start Date	End Date

Web Site:

User Name	Password	$	Day Monthly Yearly	Start Date	End Date

Web Site:

User Name	Password	$	Day Monthly Yearly	Start Date	End Date

Web Site:

User Name	Password	$	Day Monthly Yearly	Start Date	End Date

NOTES

www.ingramcontent.com/pod-product-compliance
Lightning Source LLC
Chambersburg PA
CBHW080737290526
45790CB00008B/3233